Anxiety In Rela
For Begin

Overcome Jealousy, master secret techniques to overcome anxiety and say bye bye to negative people. Fast and easy guide to live an amazing couple life

Philip Steiner

TABLE OF CONTENTS

INTRODUCTION

Thank you for purchasing this book against relationship anxiety.

It is important to note that when you continually worry in your relationship, you develop low self-esteem and, eventually, insecurity begins. You begin to see your partner's intentions or actions in a negative light; you consider your partner intimidating or critical.

To the extent that relationships are beautiful and enjoyable, they can also generate anxious thoughts and feelings. These thoughts can arise at any stage of the relationship. If you're not in a relationship yet, the thought of meeting the right person and being in a relationship can already generate anxiety for you, which you need to deal with.

I am sure this book will help you cope with your anxieties and insecurities.

Enjoy!

CHAPTER 1 - Mindfulness Meditation Practice and Its Purpose

When you start to recognize the toxic behaviors that narcissists bring into your life, it's natural to feel turned off and want to get some distance from them. When a victim pulls away from a narcissist but does not firmly resolve to cut off all connections to them, we call this "Going Low-Contact." This is the first small step towards revolutionary changes in their social and professional lives for many victims.

Still, going low-contact is like an alcoholic trying to scale back to two or three drinks per week for a victim of narcissistic abuse rather than embracing full abstinence. In some cases, it is truly the best option for the victim—for example, if you share custody of your child with a narcissist or if you are financially dependent on their continued positive opinion of you. But even in these cases, the victim must maintain firm boundaries and be vigilant of all their interactions with the narcissist not to allow any subtle or sub-textual abusive behaviors to slip through the cracks.

Remember that for the narcissist, all attention is good; they may mislead you to feel, for a time, that you have gained the upper hand in the relationship by listening to your complaints about their behavior, even allowing you to yell to express your frustration, or prompting you to "get even" with them. While you might imagine this to be painful or difficult for them, they may enjoy being yelled at because it proves to them you are still overwhelmed by the emotions they are inspiring in you. It makes them feel powerful.

They might want you to feel that you hold power in the relationship for a short time, but this is usually a tactical trick to reel you back in and lull you into a false sense of security before exhibiting other abusive behaviors. Their goal is to keep you engaged and enthralled, with more of your energy focused on reacting to the narcissist than on feeding your well-being.

Is It Time for a Change?

Victims of narcissistic abuse often feel very uncertain about moving forward because they are halfway (or more) convinced that they are the problem, and the narcissist has done nothing wrong. They have been told that they are melodramatic; they are overreacting; that they imagine things; that they are crazy; and that they, the victims are, in fact, the ones who possess an over-inflated sense of self-importance.

Maybe you've noticed your personality or physical appearance changing the longer you're exposed to this person; perhaps you're experiencing emotional symptoms that you can't easily explain, like depression, anxiety, social fear, or chronic rage. Maybe you've simply realized that you dread spending time with this person because the relationship only serves them while draining your energy.

Here is a checklist to review whenever you feel worried that a relationship might have become toxic, but you cannot see a clear solution or trace the source of the problems within it. If you identify strongly with these feelings, that is a pretty strong indicator that something in the relationship needs to change or be examined with a careful eye. Practice listening to your gut and honoring your feelings. They are not merely an inconvenience, as the narcissists in your life may have taught you to believe; your emotions are powerful tools that can help you avoid danger and find true happiness.

You Don't Know Which Way Is up Anymore

This is a common effect of frequent gaslighting. In a relationship with a narcissist, victims are often told that their accurate perceptions of reality are delusional. A narcissist might call their victim an ugly name. Then, mere minutes later, deny that this ever happened with enough conviction to convince the victim that they imagined the entire incident. Suppose you frequently leave contentious conversations with the potential narcissist in your life, feeling like you couldn't summarize the discussion to a therapist or other interested party. In that case, this may be part of the reason why. It's highly recommended that you start keeping a journal of these discussions and other inappropriate or abusive treatment; this will help you recognize and prevent the narcissist's further attempts to gaslight you and avoid accountability. It will also help you build more trust in your judgment and maintain a stronger resolve when the narcissist attempts to hoover you back into their manipulative grasp.

You Find Yourself in a Defensive Position over Reasonable Requests

Narcissists are experts at blame-shifting, which means they are great at making their victims feel self-conscious about their victimhood's realities. Say, for example, that you are best friends with a narcissist who frequently love-bombs and then discards you, showing up without invitation whenever they need your attention, but then standing you up for agreed-upon dinner dates. It is perfectly reasonable for a friend in this situation to express dissatisfaction at being stood up and ask the narcissistic friend to work on improving in this area of the friendship. But a narcissist could efficiently react by implying that the victim is somehow emotionally weak for not wanting to eat alone or needing validation. They might even go so far as to blame the aggrieved friend for choosing an inconvenient place or time to meet or having poor communication skills that prevent them from adequately expressing how important it is to them not to be stood up.

This is an attempt to change the subject or move the goal post of the argument. If you find it endlessly frustrating to try and keep these sorts of conversations on the topic with a confident person in your life, or find that you have the same argument over and over again without your needs being addressed or the problematic behaviors changing, take note of this fact and proceed with caution. You should never have to apologize or become defensive when asking for common courtesy from someone who claims to care about you, so long as the request is made respectfully. When you do, you subordinate yourself and set a precedent for others to treat you as a doormat.

You Have to Explain the Basics to an Adult, as Though They Are a Child

Do you remember Bill Clinton's impeachment trial, when the whole nation watched the president of the United States—presumably a very well-educated and socially savvy individual—ask to have the word "is" defined and clarified for him? We can't necessarily diagnose the former president as a pathological narcissist, but his behavior in that setting was certainly exemplary of narcissistic argumentation tactics. Narcissists cannot accept blame, express genuine remorse, or handle shame, so they're not above playing dumb or skirting on technicalities to avoid facing the consequences of their actions. You may be feeling mentally exhausted if there is a narcissist in your life who routinely puts you in the position to explain the rules of common human decency— for instance, why it's rude to interrupt people or that it's inappropriate to smile or laugh at someone else's emotional pain—as though the narcissist is a five-year-old who couldn't possibly be expected to know any better. It's important to note that you may also have this experience with people who genuinely do not know better, such as an individual on the autism spectrum; by contrast, though, a person on the spectrum will likely be able to acknowledge it if these issues have been brought to their attention in the past, even if they have not yet corrected the offensive behaviors, whereas a narcissist will feign complete ignorance.

When You Think of Them, You Feel Split into Two

Like someone who is head over heels for Dr. Jekyll but terrified of Mr. Hyde, you may feel as though you simultaneously love and hate this person. This is an unfortunate result of the cycle of abuse; for all the negative experiences, there are also extreme highs in the relationship, usually overshadowing positive experiences in your healthier, more stable interpersonal connections. You may also feel confused about which side of this person is real: the perfect, blameless, unimpeachable figure that most of the world sees or the monster who comes out every once in a while to terrorize you and a few other unlucky victims. Finally, you may feel split in two based on your knowledge, from experience, that dealing with them puts you in a real bind; even when you know you ought to stand up for yourself or justice on someone else's behalf, you know you'll be damned if you do and damned if you don't. The narcissist won't listen to reason or tolerate dissent, and even if you are in the right, you're all the more likely to be punished for it.

You Feel Nervous or Anxious About Situations That Never Bothered You Before

In a relationship with a narcissist, positive and negative reinforcements are doled out seemingly at random. The only logic that can be applied to the rules in this relationship is that of the narcissist's moment-to-moment desire, so you may be lauded for a particular behavior on one day and then inexplicably punished for doing the same thing at an after point. This dynamic creates a sense of constant tension in the victim's relationship and anxiety, who doesn't know what they are doing right or illegal. As such, the victim may develop anxieties around specific triggers —people, places, situations, or circumstances— feeling that, although they once were comfortable managing these things, they no longer understand what is expected of them, nor do they know what to expect from the trigger in question. Essentially, the victim learns to associate their negative memories and emotions with the circumstances, rather than with the narcissist who made a normal situation unmanageable.

You Feel Afraid of Advocating for Yourself

Some people naturally struggle to speak up or be assertive with others. Still, victims of narcissistic abuse tend to feel a particular brand of fear regarding asserting their needs in interpersonal relationships. This is because narcissists treat their lovers, friends, colleagues, and families as inferior beings whose needs are secondary; they train these individuals to fear that advocating for themselves is inherently selfish and makes them unlovable. Victims don't just feel nervous about speaking up—they are petrified that asking for fair and equal treatment will result in a catastrophic loss for them.

Spending too much time with a narcissist can destroy a person's internal barometer for healthy levels of self-esteem, so if you find yourself frequently tolerating intrusions over your boundaries and feeling afraid to enforce them, it would be wise to seek the help of a therapist or counselor. Anyone afraid to advocate for themselves might as well have a bullseye painted on their foreheads, as they are extremely likely to fall into imbalanced relationships with even more narcissistic abusers.

How to Defend Against Manipulators and Narcissists?

A narcissist will not mind your boundaries. That means you have to remember your limits. Do not give them your power. Do not get into the mindset that they have the ability not to let you do something or that they can come along and take control of them without you giving to them. They will never hold themselves accountable, so you will have to do this with yourself.

Imagine a person asking you for 20 dollars, which is all you have left in your wallet. While it is greedy to ask for this much, you are responsible as well if they do not take it from you forcibly by stealing it or robbing you. You take an active role in your life, even if you take inaction. That means you are involved in it if they walk all over you.

While deciding to become disentangled with someone who manipulates and abuses you, you must get ready to deal with the recoil that will come from this. One of the first things that will happen is a smear campaign. This is when they launch a public attack on your reputation. They are trying to get you blacklisted by destroying your reputation.

One of the most common angles the narcissist goes for in a smear campaign is to try to get your mental stability called into question. They will tell people you are "crazy" and accompany those claims with stories about you that are fabricated, exaggerated, or taken out of context. If they tell the truth about what happened, it will be a bastardized version of it.

They will also conveniently forget to mention the things they said and did during the altercation. They will make it seem like they were just trying to have a rational conversation with you, and you are losing your mind. However, you are likely starting to lose your mind due to having a smear campaign run against you.

Few things cause more anxiety and fear than being the target of a smear campaign. You fear people will believe the narcissist's claims. You do not know how far they are going to take this. You face the prospect of losing friends. You even have the fear in the back of your mind of them trying to get you medically diagnosed with a mental illness. They might even be threatening that they will cause you to be committed to a psychiatric hospital.

Let me explain something to you. They do not have the power to do that. The idea they portray in the movies where the men in the white coats break into a person's house and haul them away to the hospital for an indefinite amount of time-based on someone else's claims is entirely false. It is quite difficult to be admitted to a mental hospital willingly. Because of the number of patients mental facilities are taking care of at any given time and the limited budget they are working with, they have to be very selective about whom they choose to have committed. The person needs to be in an apparent amount of distress. We are not talking about "stressed out" or having anxiety.

The person has to be crying inconsolably or having an extreme panic attack that they cannot be brought down. Furthermore, a person cannot be committed to a mental hospital unless they have been determined to be an immediate threat to themselves or other people. If you were to tell a therapist, you have a passing thought about self-harm, they could not commit you. You would need to have physical evidence of self-harm, and a psychiatrist would need to confirm you as having suicidal or homicidal intentions. When someone is committed to a mental hospital, the process of admitting them is rigorous. You will not be hospitalized because someone says you are crazy.

This is part of the narcissist trying to convince you they are much more potent than they are. They want you to think everyone is on their side and is against you. This is why it is essential for you to band together with your friends you know will vouch for you. This is not to advise you to get into a war with the narcissist. However, they are trying to rally allies against you to make you feel alone. You need to gather your allies who will give you a safe place to land. Just being in their presence will remind you the narcissist is not the all-powerful entity they pretend to be.

That being said, it is vital not to fight them. This may seem ill-advised. You may feel like you need to go up against them to clear your name. However, this will have the opposite effect. If they are trying to establish to everyone that you are a bully and a tyrant, you speaking ill about them will confirm it in the minds of the people they have talked to.

It is very unsafe to talk to people who are your mutual friends. It may seem like they are on your side, but you do not know what is going on in their minds. They might be waiting to go back to the narcissist and tell them everything you said. They might be manipulated into doing it when then narcissist finds out you have spoken to them, and as a response, they pump the person for information. Either way, this person becomes a flying monkey.

This term describes a person working as an ally with the narcissist against you about narcissistic abuse. It might be unwittingly, but it will still be harmful to you. The narcissist will ask the flying monkeys about you, and they will also give them messages to give to you. It is a weak-minded person lets themselves become a flying monkey in a smear campaign against someone.

A narcissist uses flying monkeys to create an illusion of power over you. They get a few people to do their bidding, and then they get to come back to you and say, "See? They all agree with everything I say about you. They're backing me up, not you." When they do this, remember: few people do not mean everyone. In fact, for many people, when they hear someone speaking ill about someone else, it says a lot more to them about the character of the person who is doing the talking than the subject of their tirade. It is a turnoff for many people to hear someone speaking ill about someone else because they do not trust that person. When you hear someone doing this, you probably think, "If they are saying this to me about someone they claim is a friend, what are they saying about me behind my back?"

Also, think about this. How many times have you perceived the story of the school bully hurting someone and the bully's friends standing by and not doing anything about it? They do not even agree with what their friend is doing. They disapprove of it, but they do not want to stand up to them and have the torment directed at them. While people who let you be harassed by a narcissist behave in a cowardly manner, this shows that these people are not supporting them. The only power they have is what they have imagined.

When someone is running a smear campaign on you, it is their selves, and they will be hurting in the end. In an attempt to destroy your reputation, they will ruin their own. If you choose to say nothing on the matter, you will flip the script on them. Their goal is to make themselves look like the rational yet victimized one, while you are the crazy one who has been tormenting them. If you say nothing, stay level-headed and keep your head held high, you will be the one who looks calm while their constant ranting and raving will make its impression on others.

A narcissist conducts smear campaigns because you leaving them deals a narcissistic injury onto them. This means it is a blow to their ego. They cannot accept rejection with grace or dignity. They feel the need to get back at the people whom they feel have wronged them. It is all about getting even when you are dealing with a narcissist. You will need to prepare yourself for things being said about you, although they have most likely been talking about you behind your back all this time.

You absolutely cannot contact them while they are running a smear campaign on you. It can be tempting to contact them either angrily or with fear, but if you do this, they will share your messages with other people as evidence of their claims of you being emotionally unsound.

Gray rocking is a common term for dealing with narcissistic abuse. You become as uninteresting as a gray rock. That is where it gets its name. Stick to the facts. When they try to start an emotional argument, just say, It's your turn to pick up the kids. Don't humor them. It has become a popular tactic because you refuse to play along with their games when you use them. They want to try to get you very emotional.

They will go between trying to win you over with compliments and love declarations and responding to your rejection with insults. Many people report that their ex will message them incredibly heartfelt messages about how they would do anything to have them back in their lives when they leave a narcissistic relationship. They might send them flowers, chocolates, or other gifts that are commonly associated with romance. Some people even report offers to extravagant vacations.

These grand gestures will be coupled with a considerable amount of groveling and very poetic messages dripping with remorse. The narcissist knows how to give the appearance of being genuinely sorry and wanting to atone for their wrongdoings. However, it is quickly shown that they do not have this in mind and are not respectful of what they feel.

A person who truly is sorry for hurting another person accepts it if their apologies are not taken immediately or forgiven, but not allowed back into their lives. A narcissist's apologies and grand gestures of affection and remorse come with conditions, the main thing is that not only you have accept them back into your life, but things have to be the way they were before.

CHAPTER 2 - Cause, Diagnosis & Treatment of Narcissism

There are many challenges when it comes to the treatment of narcissism. The main factor for this is that the narcissist will rarely recognize their disorder as a problem, mostly if their tactics have worked well. Therapists find that this personality disorder's nature is for the sufferer to be very defensive and have a sense of grandiosity, making it challenging to get to the root of the vulnerabilities and problems.

Most narcissists are in denial about having problems as situations in life tend to get in their way. They never need to take responsibility for their behaviors and actions. In many respects, the narcissist is still a hurt child who has never developed healthy ways of dealing with criticism. The narcissist still acts much like a self-centered, two-year-old person.

There are theories as to the origins of NPD in an individual. Some analysts believe it is a combination of environment and genetics. It has been found that when parents of the narcissist set high standards and expectations for their child; the narcissist learns certain manipulative behaviors.

It has also been prevalent in households where the parents were excessively pampering the child or being overly critical. Vulnerability is a hurtful feeling in these types of situations, which did not help build their self-esteem. NPD has also been linked to abuse and neglect during early childhood as well.

Unfortunately, getting the narcissist to the doctor is the main obstacle to begin with. Even if family or friends could get the narcissist to seek treatment, there are no specific ways to diagnose NPD through lab tests. Only blood tests and x-rays are given to the patients to rule out any other physical issues which may be causing the symptoms.

And the other mitigating factor for a narcissist to seek help is to have a motivator. This is solely important to the manipulator's supply of attention, usually a job. Sometimes, this can also be a loved one, but the narcissist often sees people as objects.

Given the difficulty in diagnosing NPD in a psychotherapy setting, many sufferers are simply not correctly diagnosed, if at all. NPD crosses over several other types of personality disorders. There is also a possibility of the patient being comorbid, so they can have more than one disorder simultaneously. The NPD conclusion depends on a positive reaction on five of the nine models delineated in the Diagnostic and Statistical Manual of Mental Disorders (DSM-5), composed by the American Psychiatric Association (APA).

Those rules are the accompanying:

- The greed of others or a conviction that others are jealous of the person in question.

- A show of self-important and haughty practices or mentalities.

- An absence of sympathy.

- Interpersonally exploitative conduct.

- A feeling of privilege.

- A requirement for inordinate appreciation.

- Confidence that the person is exceptional and matchless and must be accepted by, or should buddy with, other unique or high-status individuals or organizations.

- A distraction with dreams of limitless achievement, power, brightness, excellence, or ideal love

- An affected self-appreciation significance.

Psychotherapy has proved to be helpful for those who have been diagnosed with NPD. It helps the narcissist to be able to treat other people more compassionately and healthily. They are also given ways to learn realistic expectations of others and themselves and self-esteem building skills.

Therapy is based on understanding the root of the emotional reactions of a narcissist. It also explains the cause and effect of the narcissist's feelings of distrust towards others and self-hatred.

Cognitive-behavioral therapy (CBT) has proven to be helpful when the narcissist is willing to change. This type of therapy can be done with a group or with family members and aids the narcissist in realizing negative behaviors and beliefs. Once identified, they are replaced with the most positive ways of dealing with life situations.

Many sufferers of NPD commonly abuse alcohol or drugs as an escape mechanism. They can also suffer from suicidal thoughts, depression, anxiety, and excessive stress. They may also experience chronic problems within the school or work environment. There are no medications to treat NPD specifically, but many are on medications for the disorder's other medical symptoms.

The bottom line is that for the narcissist to start on the road to treating their disorder, they must recognize and hate the malicious behavior and the results of their overactive emotions. They need to realize that their behavior is a choice, which means that it can be changed to reflect a healthier outcome.

CHAPTER 3 - Methods, Tips, and Strategies to Recover

Classical Psychoanalytic Cure and Narcissism

The psychoanalytic technique was first developed from the idea that the unconscious had to be made conscious, that is to lift the repression. However, just interpretations, which brutally raised censorship, could lead to frankly unfavorable reactions. An interpretation thus administered and called "wild" because of the patient's unpreparedness indeed upsets the perception that he has of himself, that is to say, his narcissism, even if the notion does not appear only later. Very quickly, Freud realized that the essential thing was not so much the fact that the unconscious becomes conscious but that it was the work that allowed this primordial awareness. The lifting of repression became the result of a particular psychic work, of elaboration of psychic conflicts. This work can be summarily referred to as a development of the ego: "Where there was the ego-id must happen."

At the beginning of the analysis, the fundamental rule was designed by Freud to favor the emergence of unconscious ideas. It is also protective of narcissism and the means to reach an extension of the ego domain.

From the beginning, you have to make this rule known: Your story must differ in one respect from ordinary conversation. While you are generally looking, as you should, not to lose your story's thread and eliminate all the thoughts, all the secondary ideas that would hinder your presentation would make you go back to the flood. In an analysis, you will do otherwise. You will observe that various ideas will come up during your story ideas that you would like to reject because they have gone through the sieve of your criticism. You will be tempted to say to yourself, "This or that has nothing to do here," or "such a thing does not matter" or "it's foolish, and there is no need to talk about it." Do not give in to this criticism and talk about it anyway, even when you're loath to do it or just because of it. You will see and understand why I am imposing this rule, the only one you have to follow. So, say everything that goes through your mind. Behave in the manner of a traveler who, sitting by the window of his/her compartment, would describe the landscape as it unfolds to a person placed behind him/her. Finally, never forget your promise to be quite frank, do not omit anything that, for some reason, seems unpleasant to say this rule induces the possibility of a regressive functioning insofar as it suspends any requirement of judgment and invites the patient to think in session as we dream to turn to his/her inner world and not to fix himself/herself on external events: thus encourages narcissistic functioning. The analysand's interest in the analyst's person, his/her love of transference, places the cure in the dialectic of narcissistic and object-oriented investments; however, that the analyst does not respond on his/her account but links his/her love to his/her precursors of the past, restores this investment to the patient's internal objects and thus to his/her narcissistic economy.

In this sense, the psychoanalytic cure is a restoration of the narcissism of the analysand.

The concern not to hurt patients' narcissism by wild or premature interpretations was formulated in the form of a technical rule: to interpret closer to the ego. In other words, go step by step and give as an interpretation only what is admissible at that moment for the psyche of the patient. One of the corollaries of this rule was the interpretative prudence, the interpretative reserve that took the opposite of the first analysts' prolixity, Freud in particular. The idea was, and still is but in another way, to extend a mirror to the patient so that he can recognize it, but without disturbing this image by untimely interventions.

The rules of the analysis framework—long and fixed length of sessions, many of them but agreed frequency, payment, and non-replacement of missed sessions, whatever the cause—are often declared rigid. This is the case, and it is their merit: they aim to protect the narcissism of the patient who can count on the duration of each session without having the obsession to be interrupted unexpectedly, or kept longer than expected, who can count on his meeting and come there even if he announced that he would have an impediment: his analyst is waiting for him. The principle of non-replacement of sessions is cautious: the vagaries of the analyst's timetable do not, in general, make it possible to replace sessions; if due to an unprecedented schedule change, the patient begins to count on this eventuality, he/she will be injured the day that this is not possible. The high frequency of the sessions—three to five per week depending on the case—even if it represents a considerable effort in time and financially, allows the analysand not to stay too long alone with anxiety raised by the emergence of 'a traumatic memory', and to experience the continued attention of someone who cares only to understand and help him/her, which in turn has a therapeutic value for narcissism.

However, the excess of the reserve, the maintenance of the analyst in an attitude of observation supposed to be objective, the excess of silence confining to the silence leaves Narcissus alone in front of a mirror which becomes a trap and absorb it in a still image, freezing the movement of analysis: "O mirror, /cold water by the boredom of your frozen frame." It is against the misdeeds of such coldness, stressing the need for empathy on the part of the analyst, insisting on respecting the patient's narcissism and allowing the psychoanalytic cure to become a narcissistically reconstructive experience.

For him/her, the analytic solution's regression allows the subject to relive the equivalent of his/her very first relationship where he/she only formed a "monad" with his/her mother. It also highlights the patient's pleasure in considering himself/herself in the mirror that the analyst offers him/her and the dimension of gift representing the investment by analyzing what takes place in him/her and the understanding that it manifests. For him/her, the pleasure is taken in this narcissistic experience, the "elation" which it procures, which is the driving force of the cure. As a result, he/she denounces the frustration that was once advocated because of an unjustifiable extension of the abstinence rule. The rule of abstinence states that no real, physical, or economic relationship (apart from framework agreements) should occur during the analysis. The erotic desires possibly expressed by the patient to the analyst (or the desire to become his devoted secretary or give him/her gifts), must therefore necessarily be "frustrated." Still, his/her legitimate narcissistic needs and his/her need for words and interpretations do not have to be frustrated.

Heinz Kohut best theorized what he called narcissistic transfers. The notion of transfer refers first to the transposition on the analyst of relations formerly lived with the patient's life's key characters. The transfer is thus, in principle, more "objective" than narcissistic. However, for many patients, the analyst's relationship is subordinated to the search for narcissistic completeness that he is supposed to provide. Kohut distinguished different cases. First, he calls it "the idealizing transference." The patient seeks to find, and in a certain way, finds again by projecting it on the analyst, the "idealized parental imago" of the past, once needed to fill the sense of helplessness and dereliction. An idealized object holding all the perfection and power to the point that "the child feels empty and powerless when he/she is separated, so he/she tries to maintain with this object a continuous union," says Kohut. Transposed into the analysis, this attitude leads to this: "In the specific regression that occurs during the analysis of these patients, the analyst becomes dependent (as a drug addict) of the analyst or the analytic procedure and (...) we can say that the condition (...) which is installed in such analyzes is truly the restoration of an archaic condition." Kohut adds "...the self of the analyzed is grafted on the all-powerful therapist..." The patient will react strongly to anything that may disturb this feeling of fullness obtained in the analytic situation. It is on these stumbling blocks that the necessary development work can gradually be developed.

The mirror transfer corresponds to remobilization in the analytic situation of the grandiose self. Still, it corresponds to a particular time of the mother in relationships: "the transfer mirror represents the therapeutic revival of the normal development of the phase of the grandiose self in which the gleam in the eye of the mother reflecting exhibitionists activities. The child (...) reinforces the child's self-esteem and, thanks to the increasing selectivity of these reactions, gradually directs him towards more realistic ways." The analyst is experienced as a separate person whose function is limited to serving the needs of the grandiose self. "As was the mother (...) the analyst is now an object that matters only to the extent that he is invited to participate in the narcissistic pleasure of the child and thus to strengthen it." The patient's profound attitude can be summarized as follows: "I am perfect, and I need you to confirm it." Assigned to the role of witness to the patient's greatness, the analyst, whose otherness is not indeed recognized, can quickly feel boredom, tension, or irritation impressions that may allow detect it.

Psychoanalytic Psychotherapies and Narcissism

In many clinical situations involving significant narcissistic distress, the classical analytic situation is contraindicated or inapplicable. This is the case, for example, when a subject comes to see an analyst because of a current traumatic situation: the unexpected rupture of a marital situation, recent mourning, situation of professional harassment, or others.

Whatever the patient's possible responsibility for the current situation, it is not time to show it to him/her. It could only be understood as "you have searched for it" and would not be of any immediate help, anyway. A traumatic condition is synonymous with "narcissistic injury resulting in psychic disorganization."

The question is to allow a reorganization, to restore investments that allow the patient to find themselves, that is to say, to find a selfish balance lost. The choice of face-to-face interviews is the one that is most often done.

In contrast to the classic analytic situation, which privileges the investment of his/her psychic life by the patient himself/herself, a face-to-face situation allows for a more significant investment of the analyst's person. The relational dimension takes on greater importance and favors an alter ego transfer.

On the other hand, the narrative of affects, often overflowing by the patient, meets the expression of a shared affect, even if it is in an attenuated mode, in the analyst. The patient can then identify with someone for whom this type of effect is not destructive.

Finally, the mere fact of settling in the therapeutic situation has a reorganizing value. The number of floating excitation decreases because the analyst becomes the support of the libidinal investment. The meanings of the traumatic circumstances about the patient's past events will gradually be addressed, diminishing the current event's impact by reducing it to realistic dimensions.

CHAPTER 4 - Healing From Narcissistic Abuse if Not Codependent

Y ou have been to hell, but how do you get back from there? What does your future look like? Can you destroy the trauma bond that you have become addicted to? What does it look like to be on the other side? Can you ever feel like yourself again?

These questions and more can come to the surface when you first manage to break away from your abuser. Life can seem strange and scary. You will feel yearnings to go back to your old relationship, even though you know all the reasons you should not. For some people, the road to healing is about healing themselves and healing in their relationships and for their partner. There is a way to do this as well—it is hard, but not impossible. You can get there with work, dedication, and leaning on others for help. Do not make the mistake of trying to do all of this on your own. There is no shame in seeking help. If you are upright at a crossroads and asking yourself: "Well, what is next for me?"

How can you heal after being subjected to a relationship with a narcissist?

Your recovery is an involved process. You know what abuse looks like from a narcissist, and you have explored the details behind the narcissist's history. You have learned who the narcissist is, what their masks are like, how they manipulate you, and you have discovered what has been happening to you. You need to learn these signs and identify the signals to prevent yourself from being placed back into a situation like this. Healing takes time and effort. You need to learn about yourself before you can heal the damage your narcissist caused. For example, you need to learn about your childhood trauma that has made you susceptible to caring for a narcissist and learning how to create and establish boundaries we need to make others adhere to. You need to understand that you are also accountable for your actions and the behaviors that you portray. This is all you will learn on your path to healing to find peace and a way forward after your traumatic ordeal. Yes, the narcissist's behavior was terrible, but you need to analyze the other half of the equation as well—yourself. Ask yourself hard to answer questions like why you stayed. Why did you allow the ill-treatment to go on for so long? Do not ask these questions to blame yourself, but just to analyze your behaviors. You are not to blame for the situation, but you need to understand how and why you stayed in an abusive situation, or even why you continue to stay if you have not left your narcissist. If your narcissist fails to get help, you need to make peace because they will never truly take accountability for the emotional turmoil they put you through. This is merely due to the way their mind works. So, you need to find closure for yourself without expecting it from your partner or ex-partner.

You will go through several stages on your journey to healing.

Stage One: Victim

When you first learn of everything you have been subjected to and realize that your partner is a narcissist, you will probably be feeling victimized. This is because you are coming to terms with the betrayal that your narcissist has created. The feelings that you have pent up inside you that add to this feeling of victimhood are:

- Hurt.

- Denial.

- Rejection.

- Confusion.

- Shame.

- Victimization by family members or friends that say you are crazy for your beliefs about your partner.

- Anger at your narcissist.

- Anger at yourself for not realizing or knowing.

- Outrage over the love that you gave.

- Anger over the time that you spent in the narcissist's cycle.

- Fear of what your following step will be.

- Fear of being in an unfamiliar new reality.

- Feelings of abandonment.

- Feeling lonely.

These feelings will run through your mind as you break ties with your narcissist or seek to change the behavior. It is a process as you have also become addicted to the way they treat you. You need to be prepared to learn about your narcissist and yourself. Once you have looked introspectively into your past and feelings, you need to study what factors made you their target. How did you allow them to creep into your life, and how did you become accustomed to the abuse? Write these questions down and try your best to answer them objectively.

Stage Two: Survivor

Once you get through your feelings of being a victim and the shock of realizing what was happening to you, you will begin to feel like a survivor. You have a mental shift during this time. Your feeling will change towards:

- Rebuilding your life.

- Seeking out a counselor.

- Being unwilling to forgive your narcissist.

- Trying to find your way back to your old self.

- Navigating through your issues of trust.

- Learning how to understand yourself and to participate in self-care.

- Re-evaluating and changing friendships as necessary.

- Your anger diminishes.

- You feel hope.

- A trigger could make you feel angry or depressed.

- Discovering your trauma from childhood.

- Creating awareness for the flags of a narcissist.

At this point in your healing, you will need to instill change in your life actively. This is where the real legwork of your recovery begins.

Before you do anything, you need to learn how to create boundaries and set limits you do not want someone else to cross. This is how you take your life back. Once you have established your boundaries, stop hiding.

Get back into routine and habits with your friends and family. Go out and have fun. Rediscover the freedom and joy that life can give you.

You might be struggling with forgiveness, which is not unusual, but you need to work on it. Your forgiveness is a pivotal step in your recovery. This act is not for your abuser, but entirely for you. You need to let go of their control over your emotions and actions.

Stage Three: Surviving and Thriving

This is the stage where you have laid the foundation for your healing, and now you need to continue to build and work on it. You might be feeling troubled during your recovery, and some initial feelings of anger and resentment might surface.

- Feelings of anger toward the person abused you.

- Unable to shake the emotions from your past.

- Shame and embarrassment at having been the victim of a narcissist.

- Lack of concentration in your life at work or even when part of a group setting.

- Feeling like you cannot move forward into your new life.

- Feeling bitter at the idea of forgiving your abuser.

- Conscious of what other people might think as they see you struggle to move on.

- Desire to move on and create dreams and live in freedom.

It is difficult to process what happened to you and to clear your mind to move forward. You need to refocus your perspective. You must learn about the dangers of keeping your emotional attachment with an abuser that you left.

There is the power to be found from releasing your abuser. Your focus needs to be on your recovery, not on the narcissist.

Find the self-confidence you are missing. There was before your narcissist grabbed hold of you. Your confidence will help you move forward. Through your confidence, you should strive to learn to love yourself. By loving yourself completely, you can wash away the chaos and anxiety that your narcissist left with you.

Change is important. With these steps, you can reclaim some of your former self while also forging a new identity for yourself. Learn to be mindful. Place yourself in every moment and be awake and active during it. As you practice mindfulness, your focus will keep bringing you to present moments, and you will be able to let go of the memories that keep surfacing from the past.

When you are ready, you can start building up healthy relationships. If you have let go of friends during your recovery, try to cultivate new and authentic relationships that offer you support.

CHAPTER 5 - Blaming the Victim and Other Stereotypes of Narcissistic Abuse

Victims of domestic violence are quite typically ashamed of what they have endured. No matter the kind of abuse endured, there are always stereotypes about what had happened and if it was deserved, and many people prefer to remain quiet entirely out of shame. They do not want to be shamed for going back to their abusers or for being in an unmannerly relationship in the first place. Many of the reasons they are often shamed are also rooted in myths and stereotypes. It is time to correct those negative stereotypes of abuse victims. After all, those who have suffered through the egregious abuse from the narcissist or other partners that chose to harm them do not need to have their validity questioned or face the shame of being told that it was their fault.

Here are some of the most common myths and stereotypes about the victims of abuse.

If You Go Back to the Abuser, the Abuse Must Not Be That Bad!

Did you know it takes the average domestic violence victim seven attempts to leave before they finally break free? When an abuse victim attempts to flee an abusive relationship, especially with someone as emotionally volatile as the narcissist, he or she enters what may very well be the most challenging time of his or her life. The most unsafe time in an abusive relationship is when the victim leaves. The abuser is far more likely to ramp up abuse if he feels as though his victim is slipping away from him, and he will do anything he can to get that victim back.

Further, there are several challenges that someone faces upon first leaving an abusive relationship. The victim may lack support from anyone, or the abuser may be someone prominent in the area, so no one will believe what the victim has to say. The victim may believe the threats or stay behind or go back to protect children, particularly if they are not physically abused. Sometimes, culture or religious norms dictate that a divorce will not be allowed. There are several reasons beyond that which may motivate a victim to go back to an abusive situation. It is not continually easy to leave, especially if the victim does not have anyone locally that can help or does not have money or access to money.

Leaving someone you love is hard, even if there is abuse involved. It is highly likely that, at least on some level, the victim loves the narcissist, and that can be a huge motivator to return as well. The victim may convince himself/herself that the abuse is not that bad or believe that the narcissist will stop as he/she has promised. No matter the reason, it is no one's place to judge the abuse victim for going back to the narcissist if that is the choice he/she has made. Instead, you should attempt to support and encourage the victim and remind him/her you are always there if he/she wants to talk.

If There Are No Marks, Then Are You Being Abused?

Abuse is not always physical, and physical abuse does not always leave a bruise. An abuser has plenty of invisible ways to abuse a victim. He/she could restrict funds to his/her victim, control communication with the outside world, threaten, manipulate, or call names. Just because there is not a physical mark does not mean that there is no harm. Frequently, the internal, invisible injuries that occur are far worse than anything an abuser could have inflicted physically.

Here are some lesser-known, invisible kinds of abuse that the victim may have endured at the hands of the narcissist:

- Emotional abuse.

- Manipulation.

- Sexual abuse.

- Intimidation.

- Throwing items.

- Damaging the victim's items.

- Threatening.

- Financial abuse.

Even physical abuse can be done in ways that do not leave visible marks. The narcissist could corner the victim and grab the victim's face to force the victim to look at him/her or restrain his/her wrists. He/she could have hit him/her, but not hard enough to leave a mark. He/she could have dumped the water at him/her or thrown something in his/her general direction to hit him, but miss. Just because you do not see a mark does not mean anything happened.

All of these actions are intended to exert control somehow, and all of them can do serious harm to one's mental well-being. The victim is at risk of developing anxiety, depression, or PTSD and is at a higher risk of self-harm or suicide.

Ultimately, if someone tells you abuse is happening, the best thing you can do is acknowledge what is being said and accept it. If the victim comes to you, do not voice that you do not believe what happened. Offer whatever support you can give, even if that is none, but never discredit the victim. It already took a lot of courage for the victim to step forward and disclose to you in the first place.

But he/she is such a nice guy—you must have done something to anger him/her if he/she hurt you.

No One Ever Deserves to Be Abused

This is so important; it needs to be repeated twice: No one ever deserves to be abused.

The narcissist thrives on making other people believe he/she is a nice guy. He/she wants everyone to see him/her as the best person ever because that is what his/her personality disorder dictates he/she should do. He/she likely has delusions of grandeur, and you think he/she is too lovely to blame for abusing someone is precisely what he/she wants. Now, he/she does not even have to be the one to gaslight the victim—random people will do it for him/her!

No matter what the situation is, no one ever deserves what narcissists do. Even if the victim had cheated or even intentionally destroyed something the narcissist thought was essential to him/her, the victim never deserves to be hit, demeaned, belittled, or abused at all.

The only person responsible for the narcissist's actions is the narcissist. The narcissist can control himself/herself if he/she puts in the effort—he/she just chose not to. Do not defend the abuser, no matter how good of a person he/she may seem to be. Of course, he/she seems like a good guy— no intelligent abuser will walk around, broadcasting that he/she fantasizes about hurting other people. He/she would never have won his/her victim over had he/she started his first date saying that he/she planned to smack him/her every time she talks back once they get about a year into the relationship.

In protecting the abuser, you are only proving that you, too, have fallen for his/her manipulation.

Only Weak People Get Abused. You Aren't Weak

This is yet another misconception. Anyone can find themselves in an abusive, narcissistic relationship, and most of the traits that attract narcissists are not harmful or signs of weakness. Narcissists are attracted to highly empathetic individuals, particularly those who are compassionate and patient. They want people who want to make them feel better, and those people are often intense and independent but find themselves entirely blindsided over time.

Likewise, just because someone has been abused does not mean that he/she is weak. Being abused only negatively reflects upon the abuser and not at all upon the victim.

Saying that only weak people get abused is akin to saying that only drunk people get into car accidents. While yes, some submissive people will be taken advantage of by the narcissist, they are not the only ones. Drunk people might be more likely to crash their cars under being drunk, but ultimately, far more accidents happen to sober drivers than drunk. Generalizations like this are fallacious by nature and should try to be avoided.

If he/she is a narcissist, then he/she has a mental health issue. You can't leave him/her if he/she is mentally sick. Remember your wedding vows!

Yes, wedding vows state of sickness and in health. However, wedding values are also said to love and cherish, and the narcissist did not hold up that end, either. Your wedding vows also never obligated you to stay in an abusive relationship that could do permanent harm to you.

Telling an abuse victim that they are not allowed to leave for any reason only makes it that much harder for the victim to free himself/herself later. Remember that statistic on it taking people an average of seven attempts to leave an abuser? That is because people say things like this to them, and they feel guilty for leaving. The victim is already likely grieving the relationship; there is no reason to guilt him/her into staying due to wedding vows or any other reason.

Yes, the narcissist may have a personality disorder, but that is not a free pass to do whatever he/she wants. He/she cannot just decide to hurt other people because he/she wants to, and his/her personality disorder says he/she tends to do so. That is hardly an acceptable reason to hurt someone. Likewise, the burden is on the narcissist to try to care for himself/herself as well. If he/she genuinely wanted to get better or learn how to live with his/her disorder, he/she would have done so. Telling the abuse victim to stay with him/her only enables him/her to continue acting the way he/she has been since there was no consequence.

If things are so bad, you could have left by now, couldn't you? Yes, in theory, but not necessarily in reality.

Leaving a relationship, particularly a marriage involving a house and children involves a lot of bureaucracy, which requires a lot of money. If the victim lacks access to money or has children, leaving is never as simple as just walking out the door and never seeing the narcissist again. Return to the first stereotype to see a long list of reasons why a person may choose to stay in an abusive relationship.

What about the Children? They Need Both Parents in Their Lives

Children need healthy parents in their lives. Growing up in an environment with two parents fighting is worse for the child than growing up in two separate houses. Even with a narcissistic parent, with one emotionally healthy parent to help guide the children through the fog of dealing with a narcissist, many children will do just fine. They are better off seeing their parents separate and not fighting, and their mental health will thank them for it. Think of it this way—if you stay married to an abusive narcissist, your children will come to internalize that as what to expect in their marriages, often taking the role of whichever parent is the same gender as them. If you do not want your children to grow up to be abusers or abuse victims, you are doing them a huge favor by getting out of the relationship.

CHAPTER 6 - How a Narcissist Gets Inside Your Head?

We're going to cover how the narcissist gets their grubby, nasty narcissistic fingers in your head and begin to move things around. If you're going to defeat the enemy, you need to know what guns he/she is going to bring to the battlefield first. Then you bring bigger guns and shields that can defend you against the inevitable, cataclysmic storm of bullshit bullets that will be fired at you. Dramatic? Perhaps, but this is war. You need to be properly prepped.

Narcissists reign supreme when it comes to being selfish. They're interested in amassing power, and more power. It doesn't matter who they have to crush, kill, and destroy o get it. They'll do what they have to get that power.

The narcissist is extremely driven for all the wrong reasons to hurt other people endlessly and ruthlessly. Mercy and remorse are not concepts they're particularly familiar with. Mercy and remorse are only ever employed as weapons— which means they're fake.

They're so enthralled with their self-proclaimed awesomeness that they never see things objectively, you see. The narcissist is the center of his/her universe—and everyone else's universe. For this reason, his/her goal is to obtain ultimate power. So, he/she will scheme, wheel and deal to make that happen.

If you keep your eyes open, though, you will be able to spot the narcissist at work (or play) very easily. How? The MO of the narcissist is easy to spot, especially once they move past the idealization phase and begin to show themselves for the monsters they are.

Here is how a narc will get into your mind and play you like a puppet on a string.

- **Devaluing you.** To recap, this is the point when they are done idealizing you and switch to making you feel like utter rhymes-with-chit. They'll mock you, insult you, criticize everything you do from the way you talk to the way you breathe, and they'll put down all the things they once professed they admired about you.

- **Triangulating.** This tactic is both brilliant and devastating. The narcissist will involve a third party in your affairs. They'll bring in this person with a "fresh" perspective on things—having groomed this person to agree with them, of course. They'll have this person validate everything that they do so that you look like the bad guy in the end. All your thoughts and actions, while understandable and rational, will be rendered invalid by this third "neutral" party. This is a brilliant ploy because if it were just the two of you dealing with something, you've still got some leeway to think that you're not crazy and your point of view has some validity to it. However, when the narcissist brings in this third party, and the third party agrees with them, then it's two against one, and you're in the minority. So you're forced to rethink your position and your actions. You start to wonder if you're not missing more than a few marbles. You must be the one with the problem, you think. The narcissist has used the third party unwittingly as a weapon against you. Following thing you know, you think you're crazy, and you begin to apologize for stuff you didn't do.

- **Displaying aggression.** Whenever you notice your narcissist is about to break out in aggression of epic proportions, what do you need to do? Get the hell out of Dodge. Why? There's research to back up that the narcissist tends to lose control of their behavior once they begin to display aggression with words. Once the narcissist begins to threaten you, make you feel afraid, intimidate you, dictate how you should connect and relate with your loved ones, and force you to do things you don't care for, then it's time for you to make a break for it. Things are only going to go downhill from there. I promise.

- **Acting like the victim.** Isn't it just amazing how the narcissist can portray themselves as the long-suffering friend or lover who has to put up with your completely unacceptable behavior? You see, the narc knows your top-down, inside out. They've got you figured out. They know their way around you like Beethoven knew the way around the keyboard. They know how to play you, so you give them the exact melody they want.

The narcissist understands all your insecurities. They know what to say and do to ruin your good mood, to make you question yourself and your abilities. They know how to pick at your old wounds until they start to gush out rushing rivers of red. They don't just know how to strike. They know the perfect moment to hit you where it hurts.

By acting like the victim in your relationship, they trap you and trip you up. The narcissist can fool you into assuming they need you in their lives. Following thing you know, they've brought up something that they know will make you feel so badly hurt. Then they'll tell you they didn't mean it, or they didn't mean it that way. And you'll believe them! Because why the heck would someone who needs you in their life deliberately say and do things to push you away? The narcissist acts all hurt that you would even get hurt about what they said or did to begin with. They get all indignant. "I trusted you enough to believe that I could say this to you with no repercussions because I thought you'd realize I meant no harm." This is what they say or something to that effect. They'll say it a lot slicker too. Those charming bastards.

- **Shaming you.** No one likes shame. It's great for keeping the tendency to act terribly in check, but in the end, shame is one of those emotions that we humans hate. It can be crippling. Now, a narcissist knows this for a fact. So what will the narcissist choose to do? They will exploit the ever-loving crap out of your insecurities and worries. They'll use all of that against you. They will make you feel ashamed of stuff that you're insecure about. They will manipulate you using your insecurities to get what they want. They'll push this so far that they utterly wreck you.

- **Gaslighting you.** When your narcissist gaslights you, they have you thinking that you're losing it. You no longer have full functional control over your mind. Your memory sucks. Your version of events is never accurate. The benefit of gaslighting you are that the narc gets to avoid being held accountable for the crappy stuff. Your reality feels skewed. Distorted. You can't trust it. You can't trust yourself. You lose the ability to tell right from wrong. In the end, you can't even put any stock in your conscience.

- **Brainwashing you.** I've got a question for you. Do you find yourself doing stuff you're uncomfortable with just to make the other person—the narcissist—happy? Do you feel like if you don't do what they expect of you, you're going to have to let them down? Do you feel a wave of guilt wash over you every time you don't do what they want you to the way they want you to? Then you, my darling, are right where they want you to be. They've gotten underneath your skin. They own you. The narcissist has brainwashed you and now believe that your entire existence is simply about serving them and keeping them happy. If you don't, there will be dreadful consequences. They will punish you, and that punishment will mar you for life.

- **Inappropriate behavior.** There's no better way for the narcissist to make you feel completely worthless than acting out inappropriately. For the narcissist, there is no line. There are no boundaries. They will keep on throwing one cutting joke after another at you and make all the things you hold dear seem like plain nonsense.

They'll embarrass you in front of your family, your boss, your colleagues, your friends, you're freaking cat—and say, "I was only kidding, come on!" So you can't even show that you're upset, because if you do, then they'll come at you with the whole "You're so sensitive" bit. Then you end up looking

70

like an uptight rhymes-with-grass-bowl who cannot take a simple joke in the eyes of others. So, you're forced to grin and bear it while the narcissist chips away at your self-esteem one cruel joke at a time.

- **Making the conversation all about themselves.** The fact is, you'd sooner be able to catch a cloud and pin it down than have a regular conversation with a narcissist. Why? They're going to make everything about themselves! You start talking about something. They'll swoop right in with their experience with the same thing and boom! They're off, bragging about their accomplishments, while you never got to finish your thoughts. It's like your opinions mean absolutely nothing at all.

- **Calling you names.** Remember when I said that the narcissist is a three-year-old stuck in an adult's body? Yeah, I meant that. If they figure that there's someone or something that stops them from being the special snowflake they are, they're going to crush it. They're going to obliterate it flat out. In the ridiculously twisted mind of the narcissist, they are the only ones right—one hundred percent of the time.

If anyone dares to suggest otherwise, they're going to get a generous dose of the narcissist's endless rage. The narcissist sinks so low that he resorts to name-calling. Not unlike a three-year-old. They'll take every chance they get to insult you. They'll criticize your opinions. They'll point out the ridiculousness of your beliefs. They will put you down every chance they get, so they can set themselves up back where they belong—on a pedestal, loved and adored by all.

- **Projecting.** A true narcissist never takes the blame for anything. They'd rather shift it onto you. Want to know if you're dealing with a toxic narc? They're going to blame you for all the things that are wrong in their life. If there were goals and aspirations they had which they never achieved, they're going to blame it all on you. They project onto you their failures.

Projection is one tool the narcissist uses to defend himself/herself. Projection is the way to avoid being noticed.

Rather than be responsible for his/her actions and choices, the narcissist will blame you and others, and he/she won't stop until you feel ashamed of yourself for your part in keeping him handicapped. Something you had nothing to do with, by the way. In the end, they come out on top, and you look like an a-hole.

CHAPTER 7 - A Path to a Healthy Relationship

Human relations are the most complex matters. There are no constants in any relationship, and what is the cause of the success of one relationship may be the cause of the failure of another, or let us say in a more precise sense that there is no clear "catalog" of human relations, especially the relationship between the two partners. Healthy relationships are clear and understandable, the details of which may differ from one relationship to another. Still, there is a broad line that makes you feel you are in a healthy relationship that does not drain you or consume your energy. The nature of personal, healthy relationships. The most important thing in human relations, in general, is the respect of all parties to the privacy of the other. This matter may be the focus of controversy in the relationship between the two partners, so what one side sees as his privacy, the other considers it his right. However, respecting the privacy space between the two partners guarantees the continuation of the relationship and makes them feel that it is not trapped. It is nice for each of you to dissolve in the other and share the details of his/her day. Still, it is illogical, for example, for one of you to impose his/her condition on the need to know the password for the other's accounts or to oblige him/her to divulge secrets of his/her friends or similar matters related to the privacy of the other. Therefore, respect for privacy is an important thing that makes the relationship a healthy relationship and not a problematic relationship that harms both parties. Read also: Things you must accept to have a healthy emotional relationship Acceptance. One of the worst annoying things in a relationship between two partners is the desire of one of them to change the other and even making the matter his/her primary goal and watching from time to time whether or not a change has occurred. It is negative. The results cause permanent problems between them. Who has the right to change someone else's nature! The other party is not entirely responsible for the expectations we have made for him/her or is obligated to change himself/herself to conform to them! It is unfair that we hold others accountable for our expectations of them and ignore their character and the details of their personalities. Therefore, healthy relationships are based on acceptance by each of the two parties to the other, or let us say that love is unconditional so that each of you accepts the other with its faults and advantages without forcing him to change. Being frank in many relationships, one of the parties may struggle to express his/her feelings or anger about something for fear of leaving the other party to him/her or for fear of a reaction that causes him/her psychological harm, so the fear of the reaction is worse and more harmful than the act itself. Still, these relationships are relationships. Satisfying is far removed from healthy relationships in which openness is an essential part. So, there is always frankness about the negative feelings before the positive ones. Both parties can express themselves clearly and frankly without fear of the results, but rather help the matter open a door for discussion. The best thing that healthy relationships give to both parties is self-confidence. Supporting other social relationships in some relationships may be a withdrawal from other relationships and social circles. One of the two parties may force the other to withdraw from them! However, these relationships are satisfactory, so one of the two parties wants to isolate the other from all his/her circles so that he becomes the only one controlling everything. In healthy relationships, each of them maintains his/her circles and other social relationships, but improves them and has the energy and the ability to deal calmly, which is what unhealthy or satisfactory relationships do not do, which may push and strengthen the desire to withdraw and the feeling that there is no energy for any social interaction. There is nothing in it but desire to withdraw and be alone. Read also: 8 mistakes that you make when choosing your partner. Unconditional support. Here, everything depends on support in matters that the other thinks are compatible with his/her requirements and the matters he/she is satisfied with only and unconditional support in anything. It may be your study of something somewhere against your partner's desire. However, you find sincere support from him/her in realizing that it is all about yours. In the end, the nature of healthy relationships imposes itself, and its reflection on you will be clear in contrast to what unhealthy, good relationships can do, which are nothing but negative feelings. After its completion, the person feels he/she will start from scratch after depleting his energy and complete self-confidence.

To maintain a healthily built relationship, there are few things that you should do and others you should never consider.

What to Do?

1. **Show your interest by preparing for the first meeting:** When you meet someone for the first time, invest some time in a quick search for them. This will help you identify areas of common interest, demonstrate your interest, and help you get what Copella calls a "first impression," as people care about those they care about.

2. **Be an active member of your relationship:** "Shared experiences are one of the best ways to build and shape relationships," Copella says. In addition to his membership in the "Young Corporate Presidents Organization," Copella is strongly involved in the Columbus community through the associations "Meals on Wheels" and "Habit of Humanity" (Habitat for Humanity), and the Columbus Chamber of Commerce board of directors. He recommends volunteering your time on a good project as a great way to find people who are "passionate and buzzing." These are the kinds of people with whom you should build relationships. "The result will be lifelong relationships," he said.

3. **Celebrate the success of others:** "Individuals have been occupied constantly, and it's decent for somebody to focus on you," says Copella. Individuals buckle down, and that implies a ton to them a great deal when others recognize the aftereffects of their endeavors. "Messages and sharing photographs of articles are incredible approaches to exhibit that you are energetic about your companions' prosperity," he

adds. On the off chance that you are truly content with your companions' prosperity, the advantage is twofold, you will impart the delight of accomplishment to them, and they will value your consideration. Cozy connections rely upon shared advantage, and the best that equilibrium gives and takes is more profound and more lasting.

4. **Be constantly present:** Woody Allen says the vast majority of life is available, yet Copella says assembling genuine fellowships, and not simply a ton of shallow connections requires consistency, by the way you are, yet in addition where you are. Try not to "bounce" all around, he says, yet "be continually present at great occasions and associations." Making a work to go to a large portion of an association's occasions has a lot more noteworthy effect than showing up each time in a better place. It demonstrates that you are not kidding about your premium in their tasks.

5. **Be deep:** "Life is short," Allen says, "Go past minor babble and discussion about the significant things." People will recall what is critical to them, so discussing the climate won't leave a follow on their brains. "I generally attempt to invest my energy talking about family, individual and business matters," says Copella. "Be a wellspring of helpful data. Offer assistance when you think somebody needs it," he adds. Cozy connections rely upon shared advantage. "I got help constructing my profession, so I put forth a cognizant attempt each day to help build up the gifted individuals around me." The connections that

78

equilibrium give and take are more profound and all the more persevering.

6. **Look to the future and don't forget the past:** While it is natural to want to build relationships with people who have already arrived where you want to be, it is also important to help the following generation get to where you are. Not only is this what needs to be done, but it will also protect you from being forgotten. "I saw many times the top professionals who woke up one day and found that all their acquaintances had retired," Copella says. Investing in relationships with people at all stages of your professional life makes your relationships complementary. Thus you are in contact with diverse age groups, and friends surround you at every stage of your career.

Each romantic relationship has a different goal to reach the ending. Still, the overriding goal remains marriage and to get happily married and have the cutest wedding ever of your dreams, bonding and building your very own family. If you are in a successful relationship and go away from the formal engagement, you should talk to your partner about these questions.

What Decides Things—the Tipping Points—for You?

We all have critical points on all issues, and those crucial points might relate to legal questions—whether you want children, though. You need to live projects you have a passion for achieving or career goals you need support to achieve. Knowing these issues that cannot be negotiated—the tipping points — will give you a good understanding of what your future life will look like with your partner, which you must know, and whether it will work for both of your opponents, and if the tipping points are compatible, your marriage will have a stronger chance of survival.

How Much Time Do You Need on Your Own?

Everyone needs time on their own, but some people need more time than others, and if you don't know that being alone is a natural need for your partner, you might assume that he/she is withdrawn, angry, or resentful when he/she is looking for a space in which he/she is alone. Consequently, establishing that both of you need time alone from the start—and how will manifest this—strengthens and strengthens your relationship and prevents confusion in the future.

How to Close a Relationship with a Narcissist?

It's over. You have figured out who they are, what they are, and you can no longer remain in the relationship. However, leaving someone with a Narcissistic Personality Disorder is easier said than done. For the most part, narcissists never change because they don't believe anything should change. So, you are trying to explain why you are leaving is not likely to sink in for the NPD you live with.

Many even go to couples' therapy, asking their spouses to change and be closer to them. They have no clue that there is no trust after years of abusive narcissistic behavior, no ability left for the spouse. Notice they didn't apologize or say they would change. They won't. So, at this point, the only thing to do is leave. However, leaving a narcissist can be dangerous. We're not saying it is every time, but it certainly can be. You are their possession. You are their symbol to the outside world of how successful they are and their good person. Anger and bitterness are likely to be their response to your left. On the other hand, you maybe dealing with a full-blown depression and anxiety syndrome after years of verbal and emotional abuse. Yes, you have been traumatized over all these years of life with a full-blown narcissistic personality disorder. Yes, you do have post-traumatic stress disorder, which will make it harder to leave, but you can still do it. In some cases, you have to do it. To stay with this particular narcissist would be death for you.

Why You Can't Leave?

1. **You believe there is hope.** After all these years of trying, giving love, and being there for him/her, you have a hard time giving up hope he/she could change and love you. As we know, narcissists don't change. They may even pretend to change or promise they will but remember they can't. Don't fall for it. Let go.

2. **The Narcissist can push your buttons—manipulate you.** We know how manipulative the narcissist is. That's a major reason for leaving—to get away from that manipulation. Still, they will tell you what you want to hear, promise you what you want to be changed and managed to push all your buttons to get you to stay. Even if they want to keep their promises to you, they will not sustain good behavior.

3. **He/she keeps winning you back.** He/she will keep doing this long after you are gone, so keep your guard up. He/she will keep using all those charming, charismatic and manipulative techniques to get you to come back. Just remember that nothing you do will change a narcissist.

How You Should Yourself Prepare to End the Relationship?

Knowing you cannot change someone with narcissistic personality disorder, you need to prepare yourself for leaving the relationship. Here are some things to organize as you prepare or shortly after you leave. You will need support to make this happen.

- Confide in a friend or family member who you know will not confide in your narcissistic spouse. You feel lost and alone after years of emotional abuse from a narcissist. Confide in someone that you know you can trust.

- Find ways to regain your self-confidence and self-esteem that's been taken from you during years of emotional and verbal abuse. Remember your self-worth and in the future, steer clear of abusive, controlling people. However, be aware that as you leave, he/she may get custody of all the friends and go out of his/her method to make you the bad guy. As someone with narcissistic personality disorder, he/she cannot be seen as the bad guy in this. He/she needs the admiration, the sympathy and the support of your friends.

- Join a support group like codependents anonymous with people who will understand what you have been through. They can help you heal.

- Put a no contact rule in place and enforce it on him/her and yourself. It takes time to heal, and if you have contact during that time, you open yourself up to being manipulated into going back to him/her. You need to have regained your self-confidence and self-esteem before you would see him/her again. This takes years, and you are better off never seeing him/her again if possible.

- See a therapist before you leave. You will find necessary all the sustenance you can get, so put this relationship in place first.

- Once you make the final decision to go—GO! Don't hang around. Don't give him/her any opportunities to manipulate you.

- Be safe. You are dealing with a potentially dangerous person. Many people with narcissistic personality disorder can be violent, mean, and you just don't know what might happen. If you feel at all unsafe, take measures to protect yourself. Have family and friends with you when you leave. In the worst-case scenario, you have to inform the authorities you leave and ask for their oversight.

- Watch out for revenge. Narcissists are known for seeking revenge and holding a grudge. Expect something and be prepared emotionally but don't let it affect your new narcissist-free life.

- Don't answer the door if he comes around after you leave. Maintain the no contact rule for at least a year if you can.

Healing After Ending a Relationship with a Narcissist

The door closes, and the narcissist is gone from your life. But not from your spirit. They do and say have a way of staying with you for a while, impacting your self-esteem even though he isn't there to do it. It was so hard to walk away, and now it will be hard to stay away and begin to heal.

The key to staying away and beginning to heal is detachment. You have to detach yourself from everything you thought you knew about him/her and everything you felt for him/her. Let go. Detachment is letting go.

- **Step 1:** Stop blaming yourself for what went wrong and start blaming the narcissist for being incapable of really loving you. See the relationship for what it was and see him/her for who he/she is as someone with narcissistic personality disorder.

- **Step 2:** When a relationship ends, you go through grief stages, just as someone died. In this stage, the anger comes. You are angry at how he treated you and angry at the abuse you endured.

- **Step 3:** This is your stage. It is about how much stronger you are now. You're thinking of positive thoughts in this stage. You feel good about the work you have done. You feel free of the love you once felt for him/her, and now you can't stand the sight of him/her. You are spending more time with friends and creating a new life.

85

- **Step 4:** Detachment! Success! You focus on yourself and your life now. You rarely even think about him/her. You are physically and emotionally free from any narcissist you might know.

What Could Have Happened but Didn't?

Understand what could have happened here if we had played out an entirely different story. The ending of the story we played out was all positive. Sure, there would be pain and grief, but you would get through it. This is not how the majority of relationships with narcissists end. Here are some alternative endings that you will want to avoid.

1. The narcissists find ways to continue to betray you even after the relationship is over, and you have left.

2. The narcissist makes false accusations about you. They accuse you of doing what they have done. There may even be charges filed against you.

3. Emotionally, you don't recover. You live depressed, alone, resigned…People in this stage lose their careers, family, and friends. Substance abuse may come into play here. You lose interest in everything. Nothing gives you hope or enjoyment anymore.

4. You get very ill from stress and depression. Far too often, we underestimate the toxicity we have been

living with all these years of sharing life with a narcissist. You hold a lot of that toxicity in your own body, and it can kill you. Stress raises cortisol levels and weakens the immune system. Stress can increase blood sugar levels and blood pressure levels. The result can be a heart attack, cancer, depression, stroke, and digestive disorders. Substance abuse and self-medication happen, as well.

5. Physical violence from the narcissist. Though most domestic abusers do not have narcissistic personality disorder, some people with NPD may become domestic abusers in this circumstance. Keep yourself safe. Be constantly aware. Live your life but don't take unnecessary chances.

6. Unfortunately, some people in this situation simply cannot handle all the stress, grief, abuse, loss of self-esteem, and they feel they have no purpose or worth left. They commit suicide. Don't ever, ever, ever underestimate the toxicity that is present in a relationship with a full-blown narcissist.

CHAPTER 8 - Things That May Affect Your Relationship

Living partnerships arise from mutual love and respect between the two partners ' hearts and souls. At first sight, some may fall in love. Others may take time to fall in love, which is more logical since it takes time to think about it and examine the attributes of the person you love. You have to know what he or she does in a bad mood, how he or she will behave in trouble and trouble, and to what degree they can affect you in argument or earnest conversation. Love relationships tend to be sweet and savory, and you believe in this. You must select, provide and authorize ten key moves or acts that can impact your relationship worse and lead to the killing or manipulation of love based on my knowledge of relationship sneak peeks, crypts, and complications.

They are neglecting small businesses and stuff. Ignoring little things and memories in a relationship will indeed torment them, as these small things are the factors that form a relationship with higher and sweeter things. For example, when you failed to announce and believe in your annual day of relationship forming, your partner could be angry, mainly if they expected you to be ready for the yearly event. Then you should focus on it, remember every small and big thing, which your partner can cheer up, remember every sweet memory, and get it live again.

- **Jealousy overrated.** This trait will seriously destroy your relationship before you can hopefully save it and repair it again. It is so bad to be so blind with your friend's actions, as extreme envy is also a matter of doubt and suspicious movements and activities in your lover. You always want to see your partner, and you never like to see him or her with others, particularly from the opposite sex. In a relationship between couples, it acts as a great danger. You should believe in three aspects to conquer overrated jealousy; your friend, self-esteem, and soul. You will have an assured feeling if you can trust in your partner because you just love you only and others, he or she wants to be with you ONLY, and they love you so much, you are a wonderful person, and you should believe and be proud of that. If you can trust in your confidence, you will be very proud of yourself and your strengths and inspire you to repair and conquer your limitations or disadvantages. You will ask yourself several questions, such as believing in your soul: is my lover a property? Yes! No! Since I can't own a human, I do not hold him or her. For example, this question will soften your overrated jealousy.

- **Summary.** One of the worst moves, if you deceive your partner, he or she will lose complete interest and more likely to break up with you. There might be just for you to betray your partner such as feeling unselfish about your partner while fearing to hurt him or her because you lost interest in him or her so that you continue with him or her in a false relationship where your body may be with him or her; however, your mind is total with another person. You must never cheat on your partner, be true to your love, wisely select your partner, and avoid being inspired by a character's externalities. Be energetic, knowledgeable, and attentive.

- **Negative indicators of mood.** All of us have good and bad times in our daily lives, but we may vary from one person to another in terms of representing a lousy mood. You can be in a bad mood, and unexpectedly, in front of your girlfriend, you can cry an unconscious word or phrase like "Get out of my face right now!" It'll undoubtedly annoy your lover who has come to ask you a question about your mood. This is also risky and results in a partnership loss of interest. Conversely, chat with your friend about your bad mood, which is why he or she will be the best listener because he or she will listen to you while trying to fix your problem.

- **Quarrel.** The noisy argument with your wife is especially an adverse move in the media; people are going to watch you, and you are both humiliated and unintentionally rude. Conversely, discuss and speak calmly, politely with your friend, raise your voice, and keep the query between you and him because these problems should be private.

- **Reads.** Lying with your partner means you're not willing to talk with your partner about some things, and it raises a question in your partner's mind: If you don't want to tell me, who will you say? Am I not your most beloved and favorite person? You know, of course, what this topic would lead to. So never lie to

92

your partner, and it will be better to say a harsh truth to him than to lie to him or her gently.

- **Ignoring your lover is one of the relationship's most fatal errors.** Whether you miss the call or your partner's message, this will be bad if you have no justification for that as a matter of urgency because it seems obvious. After all, you ignore him or her with an intention or do it because of an urgent incident that may have happened to you. Always neglect your partner, be polite and respectful, respect your lover's wishes and needs, and continue your contact with your lover to make him or her feel safe, secure, and happy.

- **Beating.** You're going to lose him/her if you hit your friend. No more, no less. This will lead to an immediate breakdown, especially when there is nothing official between you, including marriage.

- **Italian intolerance.** You may find it challenging to deal with your partner if you are the type of person does not tolerate it effortlessly, particularly when he or she repeats the same thing at the beginning that led you to intolerance. The heart is shut, and the mind governs, of course, a relationship disadvantage. To cure this, focus on yourself, seek counseling, try being a tolerant person, do Yoga. Fill your time with pure and straightforward compassion and be an intelligent person.

- **Humiliation!** Many people are so vulnerable to embarrassment. It is supposed to make you feel good about yourself in a relationship. It should increase their confidence and self-esteem. Getting prepared to handle stupid or insignificant is the opposite of a person's relationship. You should plan for the break-up if you humiliate your partner in the media. Never embarrass your friend, either publicly or in private. Please trust him or her and be kind to make them feel special.

CHAPTER 9 - Ending a Relationship with a Narcissist

Whether you are an empath, a non-empathetic person, co-parenting, or just figuring out your spouse of many years is a narcissist, all narcissistic relationships are difficult to end.

Because of the idolizing, devaluing, and discarding patterns you learned about for an empath, it can be difficult to let them go as there will always be the belief that they will change. Others may take some time to figure out if leaving the narcissist is the right thing to do while plotting, planning, and imagining life without their spouse. Those who have children with a narcissistic spouse can be extremely difficult because children are involved. All break-ups are challenging—not just narcissistic ones—but this one may be the biggest rollercoaster of your life. As you end your relationship with the narcissist throughout the process, you may have feelings of going back and overwhelming sadness.

There may be some mixed emotions and feeling relieved, but as time goes by, your mind will start to wander to the good times.

In any circumstance where an individual experiences the end of a relationship, they will feel sad, angry, and maybe in denial.

These are the most vulnerable times, where drinking or drugs can reduce pain. However, these are unhealthy habits, and instead, you could be using your time to work on yourself and overcome your abusive past by learning about narcissism and the 62.

Many roads to recovery. So, what exactly does it feel like when a narcissistic relationship ends?

Obsessing

During your narcissistic relationship, you may have spent a lot of time trying to analyze their behavior. You may have found yourself lost in thought, going over every detail of your last argument, what led up to it, and why there was no solution in the end. In the relationship, you were obsessing over your problems, and once the narcissistic tie ends, you may still find yourself obsessing over why it ended and how it got so bad. This is a habit that you have formed inside your mind, and to break it, you have to be aware of the obsession and focus on changing or distracting your mind from it. After you do this many times, the over-analyzing should stop.

Rationalizing

Rationalizing or justifying every one of your ex's behaviors can drive someone mad. Maybe you have made excuses for them or took it upon yourself to account for why they did what they did.

In doing this, you have created a pattern where you are minimizing the abuse, giving them more reasons to lie, and walking on eggshells around their egotistical nature. As you realize that it's over, you will start to rationalize again as this is the first step to healing—the denial stage. The first thing you must do to beat this habit is to cut anxiety.

Anxiety

The funny thing about anxiety is that you have to dial the anxiety back down to feel better once you are revved up. As much as this sounds like common sense, it's quite difficult to do. The more stress and tension you hold in your mind and body, the more anxiety will take over and start to control you. On top of the anxiety cycle the narcissist has kept you in, now you have a new fear of what will happen when you leave. The familiarity will be gone. There is no one to turn to.

What helps with anxiety—especially at the moment—is deep breathing and meditative exercises. Besides that, taking care of your health, like eating the right food, getting enough physical exercise, and keeping your brain active, can reduce anxiety.

Not in the Mood

You may feel as though, some days, you are just not in the mood to do anything. You don't want to cook, or rather don't know what to eat because nothing is appetizing. You may not be in the mood to talk to anyone, although a good conversation may lift your spirits. When it comes to simple chores like getting dressed, showering, reading a journal, or just watching TV, you may just feel blah, like there is nothing you want to do and think maybe you should just go back to bed. Though, too many of these days can lead to depression and even more anxiety if you aren't careful.

You will have these days and feel this way because your life isn't dramatic anymore. There is no one to please, no one to fight with, no one to scurry around for, no one to think for, etc. Instead, you are left with this hole that was filled with darkness. Try to find other things to fill that void now that you have more time. Figure out if you have any interests and hobbies. Go on adventures with your friends and learn how to enjoy life again.

Shame

Shame comes when you finally realize that you were with a narcissist all this time and ignored your friends and family who may be tried to help you. You may think about how naïve you were or how stupid you feel now. One thing to remember when shame and guilt creep up on you is that you must allow yourself the patience to feel love again. A narcissist is very good at seducing you, blinding you with their charm, and keeping you dependent on them. Understand that you were being played and that you are the victim in this crisis, not them or anyone else.

Also, it is no one's fault, so forgive yourself and be thankful that you are a forgiving soul because one day, someone will come around and make you feel blessed for being who you are.

Second-Guessing Everything

Right from the beginning of your relationship, when things were rainbows and full of stars, the narcissist decreased your self-confidence. They may have told you how wonderful you are, how you are one in a million, maybe they were looking for you this the whole time and it makes sense why no one else worked out. They showered you with gifts, praise, surprises, and possibly the best intimacy you ever experienced. Then, right when you were getting comfortable and settled in, they ripped you down by passive-aggressively saying snide comments to make you question whether it was a compliment or an insult. Because the relationship was fairly new, you let it go. After some time went by, you found yourself doing everything they told you to do, as if you were their little puppet. You built their self-esteem while they knocked you down, again and again. But because of how wonderful it was initially, you justified their actions and created a false hope that things would get back to normal if you just tried a little harder. Through this entire process, now compliments may seem foreign to you, you may look at yourself differently because of the mental abuse, and you may even question your motives and boundaries for allowing this to happen. The best way to rise above this self-doubt is to focus on self-love and reach for self-help journals or therapists to help you rewire your brain. Strive toward personal growth and stick positive affirmations all over your house to remind you that you are only human and you are growing.

Intense Sexual Urges

Narcissists use their expertise in the sexual field to keep you locked in, as sex is mostly used to blind someone through the endorphin rush to stay involved. This is why other people see what's happening long before you do. Sex is a mutual fulfillment, where you both are getting your needs and wants to be met. When your narcissistic lover is gone, so is the sexual affection. Find healthy ways to get the endorphins you were used to having. This is done through an intense workout, a night out with many friends, gut-hurting laughter, and emotional closeness with your children. If all else fails, read a romance novel and use your imagination until you can get back out there.

Envy/Jealousy

Since narcissists are very selfish and only care about themselves, they will most likely have a back-up plan. All they care about is getting their attention supplied, so if you end things, there is guaranteed another one lined up right after you. You may run everything you and them did through your mind and wonder if they miss you, think about you, or ever loved you. When you think about or see them doing things the two of you used to do, and jealousy creeps in, remind yourself to feel sorry for the person they are with. As much as they betrayed you, let you down, abused you, and trapped you, then discarded you as if you were nothing, they will surely do it again. Be lucky that this following time, it won't be you again.

Grief

Once you have finally accepted that the narcissistic relationship is over, you may feel an overwhelming amount of sadness. This is called grief. You may feel it intensely, which will make you want to beg for them back and convince yourself things weren't so bad, or it may come in little spurts when something happens to remind you of them. Grieving is the final process and may persist for years if you truly loved them. It can be difficult letting any relationship go, but one with a narcissist could be the hardest due to their love-bombing methods and their trauma-bonding techniques. Your mind will always want to think that they are not narcissistic, that they are just human beings who have good days and bad days like the rest of us. Their morals may be a little off, and they make poor decisions, but they also suffer from deep insecurities that they can't help but project onto someone else. You may feel empathy and think to yourself that you can still fix and help them if only you could explain that their ways are not their fault and you can get help. But remind yourself that you have tried these things, and it never ended well for you.

When grief settles in, comfort yourself through your sadness and realize that it had to take a narcissist to show you how strong you are.

If you are afraid that your narcissistic ex will be better for someone else and get married and treat their spouse way better than they ever treated you, don't worry—our personalities are basically like a psychological fingerprint cannot be fixed nor erased. If they were selfish towards you, they are going to be this way after on, as well. If you dwell on the fact that you heard they went to counseling to change for their new lover, it just means that they are putting on an act until they cannot anymore. If you fear you will never get your needs fixed, (sexually) like they did for you, understand that there are many people in this world with things you probably haven't even imagined that you would like yet.

CHAPTER 10 - Emotional Freedom Technique (EFT)

The Emotional Freedom method, or EFT, is your enthusiastic pressure point massage strategy that I often use in my center and most inclination to augment your psychological health. Despite the fact that it's still frequently ignored, enthusiastic well-being is imperative for your actual well-being and recuperation. Notwithstanding that you are so devoted to a reasonable way of life and diet, you won't accomplish the body's optimal mending and preventive forces if passionate hindrances hinder you.

EFT is a sort of needle therapy dependent on exactly similar energy meridians utilized in conventional needle therapy to treat physical and passionate afflictions for over 5,000 decades yet without needles' obtrusiveness. All things being equal, basic tapping with the fingertips is utilized to include dynamic energy onto explicit meridians on the head and chest as you think about your specific issue—if it's a horrendous accident, a compulsion, torment, and so on—and furthermore voice positive assertions.

This mix of tapping the energy meridians and voicing positive affirmation capacities to clean the "cut off"—that the mental square—in the body's bio-energy framework, hence reestablishing your psyche and body's equilibrium, which is imperative for ideal well-being and the mending of actual ailment.

A few people are careful about those rules that EFT depends on—that the electromagnetic energy that streams all through the human body and controls our prosperity is simply as of late getting perceived from the West. Others unearthed it unintentionally and at times presented by these strategies that the EFT tapping and affirmation procedure can support numerous physical and mental people. Presently it's the correct second likewise for you to gain proficiency with these standards. Nonetheless, recollect that, over any ordinary or different strategies I've investigated or utilized, EFT capacities. I've seen the outcomes on myself and my brain since I chose to use EFT altogether in June 2001. In reality, because of its high pace of accomplishment, utilizing EFT has spread rapidly, and medical services experts utilizing EFT can as of now be found in all aspects of the country and the planet.

This guide will offer a rundown of where and how to tap and the reasonable confirmation strategies so which it is conceivable to begin utilizing EFT right away to help others and yourself. It will likewise offer a prologue to some creative EFT plans and basics you can use.

Tapping Areas and Strategy

There are two standard districts to figure out how to use EFT: the tapping regions and technique and the positive insistences. You should be able to manage numerous issues by applying the accompanying bearings effectively.

Legitimate EFT Tapping

The central EFT plan is straightforward and by and large requires only a few of minutes to discover. The individuals that have been attempted these strategies before by an expert have a little favorable position that has indicated them the tapping things. Notwithstanding, you should be able to get these focuses relatively quick. With simply a little practice, you'll be doing each and every round in less than a moment.

Know: Although it's pivotal to tap the correct locale, you don't have to worry about being totally careful, as tapping on the overall zone is sufficient.

It Is All in the Fingertips

The absolute first thing to acknowledge is you will tap with your fingers. There are many needle therapy meridians in your palms, and on the off chance that you tap with your fingertips, you're additionally presumably utilizing the meridians you're tapping as well as the ones onto your palms.

Traditional EFT offers you tapping with the pointer and center finger's palms and utilizing only one hand. Either hand fills in as well. Most of the tapping focuses exist on each side of the human body. Consequently, it doesn't make a difference which side you utilize, nor does it make a difference when you change sides all through the tapping. As an example, you may tap underneath your eye after from the tapping beneath your arm.

I changed this system imperceptibly by utilizing and experience. You utilize two hands alongside the entirety of your fingers, so they are delicately loose and shape a somewhat bended all-normal line. The use of fingers licenses you to get a greater amount of these pressure point massage focuses. In the event that you utilize the entirety of your fingers, you may cover a greater zone than just tapping with a few palms, and this will allow you to animate the tapping focuses handily. Yet, many gain very fruitful results with the exemplary one-gave two-finger methodology. It is conceivable to utilize in any case, yet I will in general utilize my own altered adaptation to be finished.

In a perfect world, you will need to use your palms, not the finger cushions, since they have fundamentally more meridian focuses. In any case, when you have long fingernails, you should utilize your finger cushions. It's additionally prudent to eliminate your eye and arm bands, which will obstruct your use of this wrist tapping.

Bridle Solidly—But Do Not Hurt Yourself!

However, you need to rehearse a ton, not all that hard as to harm or agitate yourself.

On the off chance that you select to use two hands, I desire marginally exchanging the tapping that each hand is fairly out of stage with another, and you're not tapping on two hands all the while.

This gives a sensation rendition of this exchanging eye development work accomplished at EMDR and might have some little extra preferred position.

At the point when you tap the things laid out underneath, you'll tap around five to seven days.

The right sum isn't pivotal however should be on time needed for one complete breath.

There's most probable an unmistakable favorable position for tapping one entire breath cycle.

If you don't mind note these tapping focuses, descend your framework. Each tapping point is under the one, which should make it a snap to remember. A few journeys through it, and it should be yours everlastingly. In contrast to TFT, the course of action isn't basic.

You're ready to tap on the focuses in practically any request and course of action, as long as every one of the things is covered. Essentially, it is less complex to look over from start to finish to make sure to do every one of them.

You can see all highlight tap in the picture underneath.

It's critical to see a few outcomes, utilize these methods consistently for only one month.

I'm certain that you can see some impact from the primary long periods of practices.

CONCLUSION

Congratulations on making it to the end of this book.

I hope I've made it clear to you that tension doesn't have to jeopardize your relationship. When you overcome your feelings and use the right coping systems, you can have a healthy relationship. These adaptation systems will prevent the discomfort from causing anxiety in your relationship as well. The duty to take responsibility for your feelings rests with you as the person suffering from distress. See a specialist who can show you concrete methods of dealing with stress that will improve your satisfaction in and out of your relationship.

I hope you have found an opportunity to improve your life and live with serenity by breaking down your problems.

Good luck!

CPSIA information can be obtained
at www.ICGtesting.com
Printed in the USA
BVHW090324050621
608821BV00010B/2004